Resilience

KYLIE KNUR

WordPOWER

BOOK SERIES BY FIG FACTOR MEDIA

WordPower Book Series

It is sold with the understanding that the publisher and the individual authors are not engaged in the rendering of psychological, legal, accounting or other professional advice. The content and views in each chapter are the sole expression and opinion of its author and not necessarily the views of Fig Factor Media, LLC.

For more information, contact:

Fig Factor Media, LLC | www.figfactormedia.com

Cover Design & Layout by Juan Pablo Ruiz
Printed in the United States of America

ISBN: 978-0-9971605-5-0
Library of Congress Control Number: 2021923561

FIG FACTOR MEDIA

DEDICATION

———

This book is dedicated to my parents, John and Lisa Knur, and my sister Kassie Knur. Thank you for teaching me about kindness, happiness, and giving me the best life I could ask for. It is also dedicated to my other half, Eric Welz, who supports my "resilience" in never giving up...whether it's a good thing or a bad thing. And, last but not least, someone who taught me great lessons in life and much about resilience, Coach Jay Miller.

ACKNOWLEDGMENTS

I would like to thank Jacqueline Ruiz for making this possible and being a mentor in my career. I would also like to thank JJR Marketing Inc., Fig Factor Media publishing, and finally, my coworkers for taking this journey together.

INTRO

———

When people set a goal, they usually consider a few things:

· WHAT IT TAKES TO GET THERE
· SUCCESS
· FAILURE
· LOGISTICS

The other thing that is required but often unconsidered is **resilience**—the ability to keep pushing on after setbacks, failures, and disappointment. **Without resilience, you won't be able to keep fighting for your goal.**

This story is a collection of quotes, thoughts, and phrases that best explain my idea of resilience.

rubber : (fig.)

ly ; buoyancy

re sil i ent

(of persons)

U & C) sticky

Resilience (noun):
The capacity to recover quickly
from difficulties; toughness.

Resilience means not letting your failures control your future.

There is always light in every situation, and if you cannot see it clearly, you can create it.

A LITTLE EXAMPLE:
IF I AM RUNNING LATE DUE TO TRAFFIC, RATHER THAN BEING UPSET AND FEELING LIKE IT'S THE END OF THE WORLD, PERHAPS I SHOULD BE GRATEFUL. THOSE 15 EXTRA MINUTES MIGHT HAVE KEPT ME FROM AN ACCIDENT. LOOKING FOR A WAY TO HAVE GRATITUDE IN EVERY SITUATION CAN HELP YOU SEE THE LIGHT.

Resilient people search for the positive. CHALLENGE: Next time you are in a negative situation, take a step back and find three positives.

What things would you never have accomplished if you weren't resilient when you failed the first time?

SOME OF MINE ARE:
1. GRADUATE COLLEGE
2. COMPETE AS A TWO-SPORT COLLEGIATE ATHLETE
3. COMPETE IN CROSSFIT

Be resilient when your ideas go unheard. **They are worth it.**

Don't let anyone dull your excitement or enthusiasm for an idea that you feel passionate about. Not everyone sees things the way you do. Be resilient. Don't back down.

The inspiration for my word came
from Louis Simmons' quote,
"Weak things break." You need
strength to hold strong.

The more I considered the quote,
the more I could apply it to
parts of the world around me.
Relationships, Ideas, Goals.
Your body, Your mind, Structures.

I didn't realize until getting into this story that I've been practicing and sharing resilience for quite some time. In college, I had six roommates. When anyone would complain, I was known for saying, "But it could be worse."

WE WOULD ALL LAUGH BUT THIS PHRASE TRULY HAD THE ABILITY TO MAKE YOU FEEL BETTER ABOUT YOUR SITUATION. IT WAS A FORM OF PROMOTING RESILIENCE: LIFE MIGHT BE HARD, BUT THAT'S NO REASON TO QUIT.

The ability to be resilient speaks volumes about your character and commitment.

To be successful at any mission, you must have resilience to keep going. It is likely you may not succeed the first time you try to reach your goal.

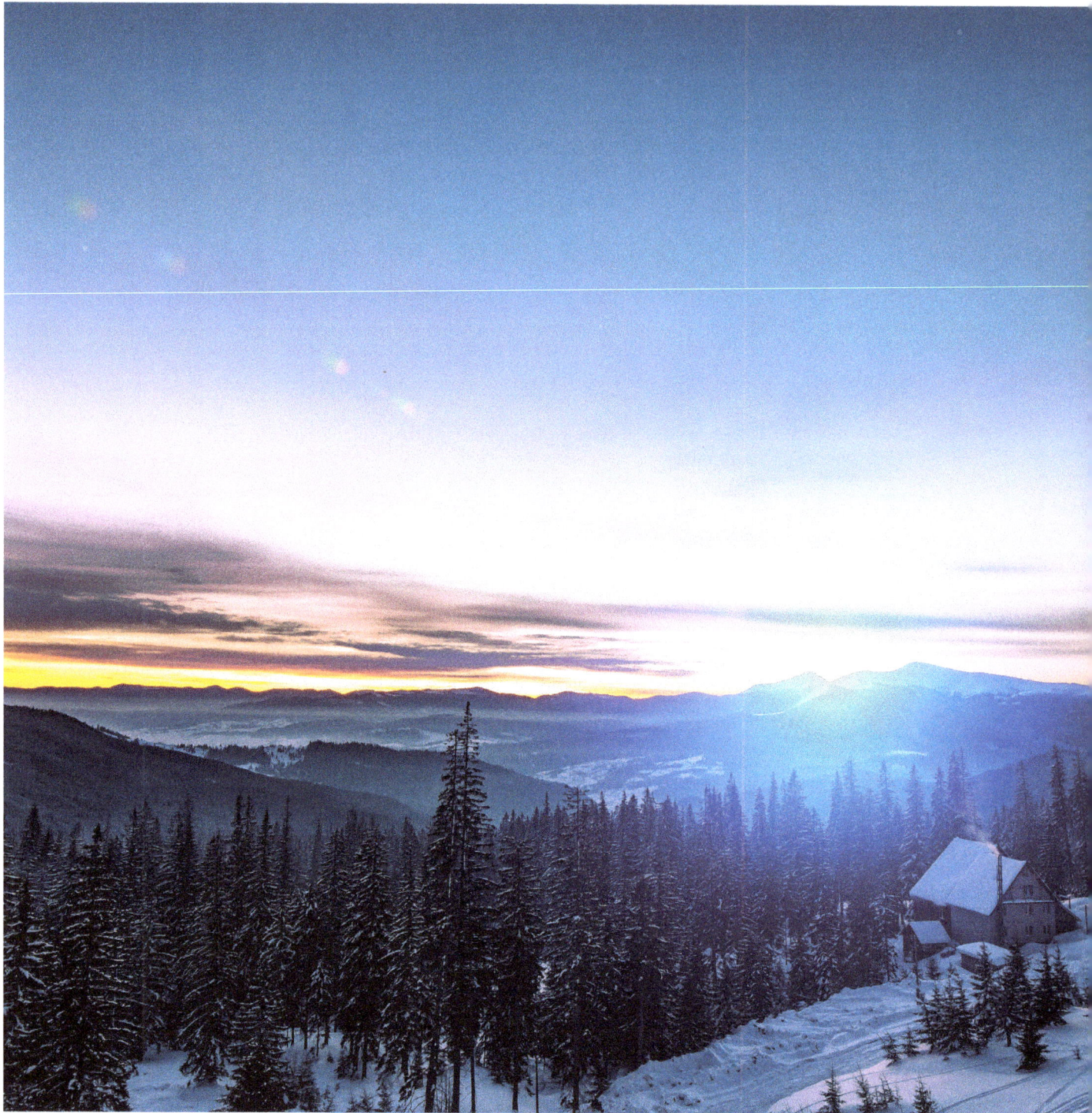

Resilience is everlasting. You will never reach a point in your life where you won't need to be resilient. Unless it is the very end and remember: resilience got you that far.

Find your purpose.
Be resilient.
Be the author.
Control the story.

ABOUT AUTHOR

—

Author Kylie M. Knur is no stranger to resilience. She has been tested in her current role as an award-winning International Project Manager, as a decorated two-sport collegiate athlete, as a CrossFit competitor, and as a student of life. In this book, Kylie shares her thoughts, inspirations, and experiences around resilience.

www.ingramcontent.com/pod-product-compliance
Lightning Source LLC
Chambersburg PA
CBHW060754150426

42811CB00058B/1401